C000148216

Pupil Book 2
Vocabulary, Grammar and Punctuation

Author: Abigail Steel

William Collins' dream of knowledge for all began with the publication of his first book in 1819. A self-educated mill worker, he not only enriched millions of lives, but also founded a flourishing publishing house. Today, staying true to this spirit, Collins books are packed with inspiration, innovation and practical expertise. They place you at the centre of a world of possibility and give you exactly what you need to explore it.

Collins. Freedom to teach.

Published by Collins
An imprint of HarperCollins*Publishers*
The News Building
1 London Bridge Street
London
SE1 9GF

Browse the complete Collins catalogue at
www.collins.co.uk

British Library Cataloguing in Publication Data
A Catalogue record for this publication is available from the British Library

Edited by Hannah Hirst-Dunton
Cover design and artwork by Amparo Barrera
Internal design concept by Amparo Barrera
Typesetting by Jouve India Private Ltd
Illustrations by Aptara and QBS

Printed in Italy by Grafica Veneta S.p.A.

Pupil Book 2
Vocabulary, Grammar and Punctuation

Contents

Using suffixes to form nouns

Suffixes can be added to words to change their meaning in some way. We can make **nouns** by adding the suffix **-ness** to some words.

- **fit** + **-ness** (suffix) = **fitness** (noun)

  My **fitness** got better when I started swimming.

- **kind** + **-ness** (suffix) = **kindness** (noun)

  The girl's **kindness** pleased her dad.

Get started

Copy the sentences and underline the words with the suffix **-ness**. One has been done for you.

1. Amara's heart was filled with sadness.

   Answer: *Amara's heart was filled with <u>sadness</u>.*

2. You can see the goodness in the old man's face.

3. She used make-up to cover the redness of her sunburnt nose.

4. The student's rudeness made the teacher angry.

5. I wore sunglasses to protect my eyes from the brightness of the sun.

Try these

Copy and correct the sentences. You need to add the suffix **-ness** to the word that does not make sense. One has been done for you.

1. I am suffering from an ill.

Answer: *I am suffering from an <u>illness</u>.*

2. Nervous is natural before a test.

3. Because of her shy, she didn't want to be in the play.

4. Some people suffer from seasick.

5. Is clever more important than honesty?

Now try these

Add the suffix **-ness** to the words. Then use each word in a sentence of your own.

1. careless

2. polite

Compound nouns

A **compound noun** is a noun that is made from two words put together. Compound nouns can be treated as one word.

- back + pack = backpack

  I carry my school bag on my back. It is a **backpack**.

- gold + fish = goldfish

  The fish is a beautiful gold colour. It's a **goldfish**.

Get started

Copy the sentences and underline the compound nouns. One has been done for you.

1. I spread the tablecloth on the grass for a picnic.

   Answer: *I spread the <u>tablecloth</u> on the grass for a picnic.*

2. I looked at my eyebrows in the mirror.

3. The lighthouse saved ships from crashing into the rocks.

4. I have a terrible headache today.

5. The policewoman caught the thief outside the shop.

Try these

Copy and complete each sentence using a compound noun made from the words in the box. One has been done for you.

| hand | play | post | sun | ~~tooth~~ |
| bag | glasses | ground | man | ~~paste~~ |

1. I love cleaning my teeth with this new _____.

   Answer: *I love cleaning my teeth with this new <u>toothpaste</u>.*

2. The _____ delivered a parcel this morning.

3. My dad put on his _____ because it was sunny.

4. After eating lunch, we go outside and play in the school _____.

5. My mum had her keys in her _____.

Now try these

What words make up these compound nouns? Use the compound nouns in sentences of your own.

1. newspaper

2. snowman

Using suffixes to form adjectives

An **adjective** is a word that describes a noun or gives more information about it. We can make some useful adjectives by adding the suffixes **-ful** and **-less** to some words.

- **care** + **-ful** (suffix) = **careful** (adjective)

  Leo was always **careful** with his toys.

- **care** + **-less** (suffix) = **careless** (adjective)

  His brother Luca was **careless** and broke them!

Get started

Copy the sentences and underline the adjectives with the suffixes **-ful** and **-less**. One has been done for you.

1. My cat is fearless and he will climb any tree.

   Answer: My cat is <u>fearless</u> and he will climb any tree.

2. My dad loves useful gadgets.

3. The bird flew high up in the cloudless blue sky.

4. This situation is hopeless. There is nothing we can do.

5. The birds sang a tuneful song.

Try these

Copy and correct the sentences. You need to add the correct suffix, **-ful** or **-less**, to the underlined words. One has been done for you.

1. The superhero was worried because his enemy was <u>power</u>.

   Answer: *The superhero was worried because his enemy was powerful.*

2. We thought the footballer was <u>wonder</u>.

3. The kitchen floor was <u>spot</u> after I cleaned it.

4. I was bored and <u>rest</u> because I had nothing to do.

5. When everyone is asleep in bed, the house is <u>peace</u>.

Now try these

Add the suffix **-ful** to each word. Then add the suffix **-less** to each word. Write sentences of your own for all the new words.

1. pain

2. colour

Using suffixes to form adverbs from adjectives

Adverbs describe how things are done. We can make lots of adverbs from **adjectives** by adding the suffix **-ly**.

- **careful** (adjective) + **-ly** (suffix) = **carefully** (adverb)

  Mr Ramdin carried the cup of tea **carefully**.

- **loud** (adjective) + **-ly** (suffix) = **loudly** (adverb)

  She shouted **loudly** so they could hear her.

Get started

Copy the sentences and underline the adverbs with the suffix **-ly**. One has been done for you.

1. She sang softly to the baby.

   Answer: *She sang <u>softly</u> to the baby.*

2. He smiled sweetly at his friend.

3. Izabel sniffed sadly as she sat alone.

4. Calum stood up bravely in assembly.

5. He spoke about his life honestly.

Try these

Make adverbs from the adjectives by adding the suffix **-ly**. Then write sentences of your own with the new words. One has been done for you.

1. rude

   Answer: *She stared <u>rudely</u> at the man.*

2. secret

3. quiet

4. gentle

5. bad

Now try these

Rewrite the sentences, adding adverbs with **-ly** to improve them.

1. The lady spoke to the children.

2. The children watched the film.

3. The man crossed the road.

Using suffixes in adjectives

Adjectives can be used to compare people or things. We can add the suffixes **-er** and **-est** to adjectives to do this. We use **the** with adjectives with the suffix **-est**.

- Javier was tall. Fortis was **taller**. Amelia was **the tallest**.

- Those books are cheap. That book is **cheaper**. This book is **the cheapest**.

Get started

Copy the sentences and underline the comparing adjectives. One has been done for you.

1. In England, July is warmer than January.

   Answer: *In England, July is <u>warmer</u> than January.*

2. Sally is the tallest student in our class.

3. Your hands feel colder than my hands.

4. Our house is the smallest on the street.

5. That car is cheaper than this car.

Try these

Copy and complete each sentence using one comparison from the box. One has been done for you.

1. Sienna tried _____ than Jo did.

   Answer: *Sienna tried harder than Jo did.*

2. The butterfly is even _____ than the flower!

3. Are alligators _____ than crocodiles?

4. Mrs Sanchez's voice is _____ than Mr Rodrigues' voice.

5. The kitten is _____ than the cat.

| harder / more hard |
| beautifuller / more beautiful |
| dangerouser / more dangerous |
| louder / more loud |
| naughtier / more naughty |

Now try these

Add the suffixes **-er** and **-est** to these words. Then write comparing sentences of your own with the new words.

1. big

2. angry

Co-ordinating conjunctions

Co-ordinating conjunctions can join two independent sentences. Co-ordinating conjunctions include **and**, **or** and **but**.

- I like fruit **and** I enjoy sweets.
- I can play football **or** I can go swimming.
- I have my coat **but** I forgot my hat.

Get started

Copy the sentences and underline the co-ordinating conjunctions. One has been done for you.

1. We could watch tennis or we could watch cartoons.

   Answer: *We could watch tennis <u>or</u> we could watch cartoons.*

2. I am tired but I don't want to go to bed.

3. They put their pens away and they closed their books.

4. They could have cheese or they could have tuna.

5. I had a new toy but my sister broke it.

Try these

Put the words in the correct order to make sentences. One has been done for you.

1. or play could inside we could We outside. play

   Answer: *We could play inside or we could play outside.*

2. but I would to like outside play raining. is it

3. or choose We apples. could choose we could oranges

4. but sleepover. party I'll a I have a have won't

5. and dad is My is snoring. sleeping he

Now try these

Join each pair of sentences with the best co-ordinating conjunction: **and**, **or** or **but**.

1. I like carrots. I do not like peppers.

2. I could play on the swings first. I could play on the slide first.

Subordinating conjunctions

Subordinating conjunctions can join sentences if the second sentence relies on the first sentence for its meaning. These are subordinating conjunctions: **because**, **if**, **when** and **that**.

- I love my birthday **because** people give me presents.

- You can get cold **if** you forget to wear a coat.

- I never cry **when** I fall off my bike.

- I promised my mum **that** I would play carefully.

Get started

Copy the sentences and underline the subordinating conjunctions. One has been done for you.

1. I am at Grandma's house because Mum is working.

Answer: *I am at Grandma's house <u>because</u> Mum is working.*

2. I am happy that the sun is shining.

3. They went to bed when it got dark.

4. I have an apple for breakfast because I love fruit.

5. I will play with her if she is kind.

Try these

Copy and complete the sentences using **because**, **if**, **when** or **that**. One has been done for you.

1. I said _____ Jamal could borrow my red pen.

    Answer: *I said that Jamal could borrow my red pen.*

2. It is warmest in England _____ it is summer.

3. I can have a party next week _____ I am good.

4. My dad is napping _____ he is tired.

5. Our teacher told us _____ we had passed our test.

Now try these

Finish these sentences by adding extra information after the subordinating conjunction.

1. You will get hot if . . .

2. I was late because . . .

3. We could go out to play when . . .

4. Sidney told his dad that . . .

Expanded noun phrases

We can use words called **adjectives** to describe **nouns**. We can also add descriptive details after nouns.

- dog
- the dog
- the happy dog
- the happy dog on the lead

Get started

Copy the sentences and underline the noun that we are describing. One has been done for you.

1. the glass vase

   Answer: *the glass <u>vase</u>*

2. the purple jumper

3. the useful little gadget

4. the house with the creaking door

5. that cheerful little girl in the nursery

Try these

Copy and complete each sentence by choosing the best words from the box. One has been done for you.

1. I would like a _____ drink.

   Answer: *I would like a refreshing drink.*

refreshing / rainy

2. We have bought a _____ game.

3. We played in the _____ field.

4. My dad is riding the bike _____.

5. My friend Lucy is the dancer _____.

woolly / new
muddy / clever
with the red basket / that is sad
talented / with the curly hair

Now try these

Describe these nouns using adjectives to give extra information. Then use them in sentences of your own.

1. car

2. chair

Sentence types: statements

A **statement** tells us a fact. Statements should end with a full stop.

- The horse jumped over the fence.

- I love eating chocolate.

Get started

Read the pairs of sentences. They do not have any punctuation at the end. Copy the sentence that is a statement and add the full stop. One has been done for you.

1. **a)** The cow was grazing on the green grass

   b) Was the cow grazing on the green grass

   Answer: *The cow was grazing on the green grass.*

2. **a)** Were the birds singing sweetly

   b) The birds were singing sweetly

3. **a)** Rabbits hopping joyfully

   b) The rabbits are hopping joyfully

4. **a)** The farmer was mowing the field

   b) Was the farmer mowing the field

Try these

Put the words and full stops in the correct order to make statements. One has been done for you.

1. started onto the fall to field rain . The

   Answer: *The rain started to fall onto the field.*

2. on farmer the . The in mowing rain carried

3. stood . tree cow stay under The to a dry

4. rabbits has in that hutch Carl live . a

5. went he The back warm hole . his so keep to mouse could

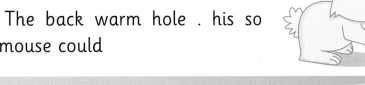

Now try these

Write a statement about each topic. Think carefully about word order and remember to use the correct punctuation.

1. Something you see on the way to school

2. Something you do in the morning

Sentence types: questions

Questions ask for information. They often use question words like **why**, **what**, **where**, **how**, **who** and **when**. Questions should end with a question mark.

- **What** do cows eat**?**

- **How** much grass is there**?**

Get started

Read the pairs of sentences. Copy the sentence that is a question and add the question mark. One has been done for you.

1. a) Was the farmer in the field

   b) The farmer was in the field

   Answer: *Was the farmer in the field?*

2. a) He was where the horses are

   b) Where was he

3. a) Nobody knew how cold he felt

   b) How did he feel

4. a) Was there lots of work to do

   b) There was lots of work to do

Try these

Put the words in the correct order to make questions. Use a capital letter for the first word of each question and add the question mark. One has been done for you.

1. cat was the where

   Answer: *Where was the cat?*

2. did what sheep the do

3. horses in many the how are barn

4. the blow did wind start when to

5. farmer did why carry the on in cold the working

Now try these

Write a question asking about these characters. Think carefully about word order and remember to use the correct punctuation.

1. A jolly baker

2. A tall teacher

Sentence types: exclamations

Exclamations are sentences that we say or read loudly or with lots of feeling. They can show anger, frustration, shock, pain, surprise or excitement. Exclamations should end with an exclamation mark.

- That hurts!

- I scored three goals today!

Get started

Copy the sentence in each pair that is more likely to be an exclamation and add the exclamation mark. One has been done for you.

1. a) You broke my laptop

   b) Theo broke a laptop last week

   Answer: *You broke my laptop!*

2. a) I can't believe my luck

   b) Was I lucky

3. a) Did you kick me

   b) You kicked me

Try these

Put the words in the correct order to make exclamations. Use a capital letter for the first word of each exclamation and add the exclamation mark. One has been done for you.

1. snow weeks the stop for didn't

   Answer: *The snow didn't stop for weeks!*

2. loud such was noise that a

3. is freezing it absolutely

4. heart racing my is

5. just it joke was all a

Now try these

Write an exclamation about these topics. Think carefully about what feelings your exclamations express and remember to use the correct punctuation.

1. A sudden, scary noise in the dark

2. A nice surprise

Sentence types: commands

Commands tell someone to do something. They use 'bossy' words called **imperative** verbs. Often, the verb is at the beginning of the sentence. Commands are the only sentence type that can have only one word. They can end with a full stop or an exclamation mark.

- Eat your dinner.

- Be quiet!

- Stop!

Get started

Copy the sentences and underline the imperative verbs. One has been done for you.

1. Cut the paper carefully.

   Answer: <u>Cut</u> the paper carefully.

2. Write the date.

3. Listen to the teacher!

4. Now change your clothes for PE.

5. Please pack your bag.

Try these

Complete the commands with a suitable imperative verb.
One has been done for you.

1. _____ your book every night.

Answer: <u>Read</u> your book every night.

2. _____ your times tables.

3. _____ a cake for the party.

4. Please _____ a thank you letter to your aunt.

5. If you are cold, _____ on a warm jumper.

Now try these

Write a command for the situations. Remember to use imperative verbs.

1. Playing football

2. Making a model

Present tense and past tense

Verbs are words that show the action in a sentence. Verbs in the present tense are commonly used to describe a habit or state that is true now.

- I **play** basketball.

If a sentence is in the **past tense**, the action has already happened.

- I **played** basketball.

Get started

Copy the sentences. Underline the verbs in the present tense once. Underline the verbs in the past tense twice. One has been done for you.

1. I dance to the music that Henry recorded.

   Answer: I <u>dance</u> to the music that Henry <u>recorded</u>.

2. I use Mum's computer these days because mine broke.

3. She ironed the shirts that I need for school.

4. We sailed on the lake all last summer and now we know it well.

5. I am nervous of the dog because it bit me last week.

Try these

Copy and complete each sentence by choosing the correct verb tense from the box. One has been done for you.

1. Yesterday we _____ a really long way.

walk / walked

Answer: *Yesterday we <u>walked</u> a really long way.*

2. If I close my eyes tightly, I _____ bright spots.

3. It _____ all day last Sunday.

4. Alexa _____ every time she reads that book.

5. Last night, Mea _____ a great film on TV.

see / saw
rains / rained
cries / cried
watch / watched

Now try these

Rewrite the sentences, changing them into the past tense.

1. Nina's grandfather waits for her to come home from school.

2. The boy runs through the dark woods quickly.

Progressive verb forms in the present tense and past tense

The **tense** of a **verb** tells you about the time an action takes place. **Progressive** verb tenses show that things **progress** over time.

Present progressive verbs show that something is still happening.

- I **am eating** the cake.

Past progressive verbs show that something was happening in the past but is not happening any more.

- I **was eating** the cake.

Get started

Copy the sentences and underline the words that make up the verb. Then label them 'present progressive' or 'past progressive'. One has been done for you.

1. Nafeesa was melting the chocolate for the cake.

   Answer: *Nafeesa <u>was melting</u> the chocolate for the cake. past progressive*

2. Amalia is riding her bike.

3. Salma was singing a song.

4. Javid was writing a letter.

5. Zahir is eating a salad.

Try these

Copy and complete each sentence by choosing the correct verb form from the box. One has been done for you.

1. While his dad cooked, Miguel
   _____ the bathroom.

is cleaning /
was cleaning

   Answer: *While his dad cooked,*
   Miguel <u>was cleaning</u> the bathroom.

2. Jimi is tired so he _____ on the comfortable sofa.

is relaxing /
was relaxing

3. Mum _____ the garden the whole of last weekend.

is digging /
was digging

4. Brigitte _____ silly faces at the baby and he started to cry.

is making /
was making

Now try these

Rewrite the sentences below twice: once using the present progressive and once using the past progressive. Think carefully about how to change the verbs.

1. Angela cleans the house.
2. Toby cuts up the paper.

Commas in lists

Commas can be used to separate the different items in a list. However, we do not use a comma between the last two items; we use **and** instead.

- I like fish, chips **and** peas.

- I enjoy running, swimming, climbing **and** dancing.

Get started

Copy the sentences. If the comma has been used correctly in a sentence, label it 'correct'. If the comma has been used incorrectly in a sentence, label it 'incorrect'.
One has been done for you.

1. Dad asked me to tidy up dust polish and vacuum the carpet.

   Answer: *Dad asked me to tidy up dust polish and vacuum the carpet. incorrect*

2. We went to the park, the shop, the garage and the bank.

3. I saw monkeys, giraffes, elephants and hippos.

4. I am wearing trousers, a shirt a jumper and a tie.

5. I play netball, football, cricket, and rounders.

Try these

Copy the sentences and add the correct punctuation. One has been done for you.

1. I would like to go to France America Spain and Germany.

    Answer: *I would like to go to France, America, Spain and Germany.*

2. My school bag is red yellow orange and pink.

3. I played with Fern Sita Henri and Morgan.

4. We have kittens fish gerbils and hamsters as pets.

5. I have spelling reading art and maths for homework.

Now try these

Copy and complete the sentences with your own lists. Use the word **and** correctly and the correct punctuation.

1. The people in my family are . . .

2. The places I would like to visit are . . .

Apostrophes for omission

We can use an **apostrophe** (') to show **omission**. This is when letters are missed out. When we use an apostrophe to show omission, we write two words as one word; this is shorter and more informal than writing two whole words.

- The words **are not** can be written as **aren't**.

- The words **you are** can be written as **you're**.

Get started

Copy the sentences and underline the words that have been shortened. One has been done for you.

1. I'm late!

   Answer: <u>I'm</u> late!

2. We're going to the park.

3. She's doing a great job.

4. You shouldn't talk during a test.

5. I hadn't thought about that.

Try these

Match the shortened words to the whole words. One has been done for you.

Answer: *1 – d*

1. *he's*   **a)** was not

2. they'd   **b)** could not

3. wasn't   **c)** they had

4. they've   **d)** *he is*

5. couldn't   **e)** they have

Now try these

Rewrite the sentences using apostrophes to shorten the underlined words.

1. <u>She is</u> a talented dancer.

2. <u>We had</u> better hurry up.

Apostrophes for possession

We can use an **apostrophe** (') with the letter **s** to show **possession**. This is when something **belongs** to someone or something else.

- **Luke's** shoes were muddy.

- The **dog's** bowl is full of water.

Get started

Copy the sentences and underline the name of the person who owns something. One has been done for you.

1. Marie's book was full of drawings.

   Answer: <u>Marie's</u> book was full of drawings.

2. I like Zayn's new toy.

3. Roger's bike is bright red.

4. This is Denise's cardigan.

5. Niccolo played with Dylan's baking set.

Try these

Copy and complete the sentences by adding apostrophes to the underlined words. One has been done for you.

1. <u>Martias</u> bag is blue.

Answer: <u>Martia's</u> *bag is blue.*

2. The <u>dogs</u> ears are black but its face is white.

3. I used <u>Matteos</u> new pen.

4. Mike is reading <u>Tristans</u> book about sharks.

5. Has anyone seen one of <u>Graces</u> orange trainers?

Now try these

Rewrite the phrases using an apostrophe. One has been done for you.

1. the blanket belonging to the cat

Answer: *the cat's blanket*

2. the pen belonging to Miguel

3. the maths homework belonging to Lily